THE KWANZAA EXPERIENCE

A BOU-GHETTO TRANSLATION

Edited by Maya Bechi, M.ED

Contributors: Donovan Bechi &
Marielle Bechi

™

THE **KWANZAA** EXPERIENCE™

A BOU-GHETTO TRANSLATION

DEDICATED TO: _____

ESTABLISHED ON THIS DATE: _____

Robson and Puritan
P.O. Box 1107
Cypress, TX 77410-1107

Published in the United States by Robson and Puritan

ISBN: 979-8-9864813-8-8
www.robsonandpuritan.com
Book design by Donovan J. Bechi with Canva

MOJA!   KUJICHAGULIA!   UJIMA!   UJAMAA!   NIA!   KUUMBA!   IMANI!

THE **KWANZAA**

EXPERIENCE

A BOU-GHETTO TRANSLATION

A NOTE FROM MAYA

What is the definition of being black? For a myriad of reasons that other people have identified, based on the labels they carry around, you'll get a different answer. That's why I am so grateful for the offensively rowdy way the younger generations are showing up. They are more likely to challenge and rebel against labels. We need label rebels. We need the changemakers, researchers, inquisitors and innovators.

If you look across the history of movements and civilizations, you will see highs and lows of unrest, uncertainty, scarcity and rebellion, peace, settlement, triumph and growth. This 2nd edition of The Kwanzaa experience is my personal journey with life coming out of a *low*, and using a controversial holiday as my rod and my staff along the way. I desired a change, I wanted joy and I was curious about Kwanzaa. My biggest question was "will this level of *blackness* fit me?" I wasn't from an upper class black family and I didn't attend an HBCU nor was I AME. I didn't have professors who'd spent time on the continent of Africa. Would I qualify? The answer is...*no*.

Because I didn't do Kwanzaa "correctly".

So this book is a step towards change making, inquiring and daring to try to innovate. I dedicate this to all of us who delight in, or are wanting to delight in the joy of being black in America. By your own definition.

Join me @thekwanzaaexperience on Instagram.
Peace & Blessings, Maya

CONTENTS

JMOJA!   KUJICHAGULIA!   UJIMA!   UJAMAA!   NIA!   KUUMBA!   IMANI!

THE KWANZAA EXPERIENCE

A BOU-GHETTO TRANSLATION

TRADITIONAL

PREPARATION

Kwanzaa is a 7 day celebration that begins on December 26th with the last day observed on January 1st. By design, each day has a significant and special intention.
Begin by familiarizing yourself with the intent for each principle for each day as this will help guide you while preparing to enjoy the celebration.

26th - **Umoja** - Unity
27th - **Kujichagulia** - Self Determination
28th - **Ujima** - Collective work and Responsibility
29th - **Ujamaa** - Cooperative Economics
30th - **Nia** - Purpose
31st - **Kuumba** - Creativity
1st - **Imani** - Faith

PRINCIPLES & INTENTIONS

Umoja - To strive for and maintain **unity** in the family, community, nation and race. (light the black candle)

Kujichagulia - To define ourselves, name ourselves, create for ourselves, and speak for ourselves. Increasing our **self-determination**. (light a red or green candle)

Ujima - To build and maintain our community together and make our brothers' and sisters' problems our problems and solve them together. Establish **collective work and responsibility**.
(light a red or green candle)

Ujamaa - To build and maintain our own stores, shops, and other businesses and to profit from them together. Participate in **cooperative economics.** (light a red or green candle)

Nia - To make our collective vocation the building and developing of our community in order to restore our people to their traditional greatness. Pursuit of a common **purpose**. (light a red or green candle)

Kuumba - To always do as much as we can, in the way we can, in order to leave our community more beautiful and beneficial than we inherited it. Use our **Creativity.** (light a red or green candle)

Imani - To believe with all our heart in ourselves, our people, our parents, our teachers, our leaders, and the righteousness and victory of our struggle. Become established and rooted in **Faith.** (light remaining candle)

LIBATIONS

A libation statement called "Tamshi la Tambiko" is recited, during which time water from the communal cup ("Kikomba Cha Umoja) is poured in the four directions, north, south, east and west, in memory of loved ones who have passed away. The cup is then passed among the group. Kwanzaa libation statement, "Tamshi la tambiko"

- For the Motherland, cradle of civilization.
- For the ancestors and their indomitable spirit.
- For the elders from whom we can learn much.
- For our youth who represent the promise for tomorrow.
- For our people, the original people.
- For our struggle and in remembrance of those who have struggled on our behalf.
- For Umoja, the principle of unity, which should guide us in all that we do.
- For the creator who provides all things great and small.

The ceremony ends with the "Kutoa Majina" (calling the names of family ancestors and Black heroes) and the "Tamshi la Tutaonana" ("Farewell Statement").

POUR OUT A LITTLE LIQUOR

You can prepare a statement in advance, or be spontaneous for this ceremony. While you recite a prayer or read a dedication, the Unity Cup is poured out in memory of loved ones who have passed away. The cup is then passed among the group. Everyone who wants to take a turn pouring out may do so.

You may also use an alcoholic beverage. But that can be expensive. This is also a good time to speak affirmations or prayers for the group or for the individuals present.

The ceremony ends with the calling the names of family ancestors and Black heroes.

THE DAILY CELEBRATIONS

26TH

UMOJA

Umoja - To strive for and maintain **unity** in the family, community, nation and race. (light the black candle)

1. Gather everyone together.
2. Eldest person (or leader): "Habari gani?" (*what's happening?*)
3. Everyone: "Umoja!" (*unity!*)
4. Pray
5. Everyone: "Harambe!" (*let's pull together!*)
6. Pour out libations
7. The youngest lights the black candle on the Kinara.
8. Discuss unity, tell a story, read an excerpt from a book or publication, sing or listen to a song.
   Song Recommendation: "Impossible is Possible" by Black Violin
9. 1 gift can be exchanged now (or wait until Jan 1st)

26TH
DAY FOR A TRUCE

Truce - To strive for and maintain **unity** in the family, community, nation and race.
(light the black candle)

1. Host a get together or celebrate solo.
2. Choose someone to be the MC. (If possible, choose the oldest person)
3. The MC prays for everyone.
4. Huddle up and say "truce"
5. The MC pours out a little liquor (or water)
6. The MC directs the youngest person to light the black candle
7. Discuss having a truce and what it will take, tell a story, read an excerpt from a book or publication, sing or listen to a song.
8. 1 gift can be exchanged now (or wait until Jan 1st)

27TH
KUJICHAGULIA

Kujichagulia - To define ourselves, name ourselves, create for ourselves, and speak for ourselves. Increasing our **self-determination**. (light a red or green candle)

1. Gather everyone together.
2. Eldest person (or leader): "Habari gani?" (what's happening?)
3. Everyone: "Kujichagulia!" (self-determination!)
4. Pray
5. Everyone: "Harambe!" (let's pull together!)
6. Pour out libations
7. The youngest uses the black candle to light the next candle on the Kinara.
8. Discuss Kujichagulia, tell a story, read an excerpt from a book or publication, sing or listen to a song.
   Song Recommendation: "Through the Dark" by FaceSoul aka Faisal Salah
9. 1 gift can be exchanged now (or wait until Jan 1st)

27TH
NICK NAMED

Nick Named - To define ourselves, name ourselves, create for ourselves, and speak for ourselves. Increasing our **self-determination**.
(light a red or green candle)

1. Host a get together or celebrate solo.
2. Choose someone to be the MC. (If possible, choose the oldest person)
3. The MC prays for everyone.
4. Huddle up and say "nick name"
5. The MC pours out a little liquor (or water)
6. The MC directs the youngest person to use the black candle to light the next candle.
7. Discuss speaking up, being true to self, defying stereotypes, creating something we can own, tell a story, read an excerpt from a book or publication, sing or listen to a song.
8. 1 gift can be exchanged now (or wait until Jan 1st)

28TH

UJIMA

Ujima - To build and maintain our community together and make our brothers' and sisters' problems our problems and solve them together. Establish **collective work and responsibility**.
(light a red or green candle)

1. Gather everyone together.
2. Eldest person (or leader): "Habari gani?" (what's happening?)
3. Everyone: "Ujima!"
4. Pray
5. Everyone: "Harambe!" (let's pull together!)
6. Pour out libations
7. The youngest uses the black candle to light the next candle on the Kinara.
8. Discuss Ujima, tell a story, read an excerpt from a book or publication, sing or listen to a song.
   Song Recommendation: "Glory" by John Legend
9. 1 gift can be exchanged now (or wait until Jan 1st)

28TH
PLAY COUSIN

Play Cousin- To build and maintain our community together and make our brothers' and sisters' problems our problems and solve them together. Establish **collective work and responsibility**.

(light a red or green candle)

1. Host a get together or celebrate solo.
2. Choose someone to be the MC. (If possible, choose the oldest person)
3. The MC prays for everyone.
4. Huddle up and say "Cuzzin!"
5. The MC pours out a little liquor (or water)
6. The MC directs the youngest person to use the black candle to light the next candle.
7. Discuss how everyone is doing, which things can be solved better by chipping in, tell a story, read an excerpt from a book or publication, sing or listen to a song.
8. 1 gift can be exchanged now (or wait until Jan 1st)

29TH

UJAMAA

Ujamaa - To build and maintain our own stores, shops, and other businesses and to profit from them together. Participate in **cooperative economics.** (light a red or green candle)

1. Gather everyone together.
2. Eldest person (or leader): "Habari gani?" (what's happening?)
3. Everyone: "Ujamaa!"
4. Pray
5. Everyone: "Harambe!" (let's pull together!)
6. Pour out libations
7. The youngest uses the black candle to light the next candle on the Kinara.
8. Discuss Ujamaa, tell a story, read an excerpt from a book or publication, sing or listen to a song.
   Song Recommendation: "We're a Winner" by Curtis Mayfield
9. 1 gift can be exchanged now (or wait until Jan 1st)
10. Decide to increase purchases made with black owned businesses.

29TH
BUY ALL BLACK

Buy Black - To build and maintain our own stores, shops, and other businesses and to profit from them together. Participate in **cooperative economics.**

(light a red or green candle)

1. Host a get together or celebrate solo.
2. Choose someone to be the MC. (If possible, choose the oldest person)
3. The MC prays for everyone.
4. Huddle up and say "Black Bag!"
5. The MC pours out a little liquor (or water)
6. The MC directs the youngest person to use the black candle to light the next candle.
7. Discuss elevating black business, eradicating "low quality" myth, share products, tell a story, read an excerpt from a book or publication, sing or listen to a song.
8. 1 gift can be exchanged now (or wait until Jan 1st)

30TH

NIA

Nia - To make our collective vocation the building and developing of our community in order to restore our people to their traditional greatness. Pursuit of a common **purpose**. (light a red or green candle)

1. Gather everyone together.
2. Eldest person (or leader): "Habari gani?" (what's happening?)
3. Everyone: "Nia!"
4. Pray
5. Everyone: "Harambe!" (let's pull together!)
6. Pour out libations
7. The youngest uses the black candle to light the next candle on the Kinara.
8. Discuss Nia, tell a story, read an excerpt from a book or publication, sing or listen to a song.
    Song Recommendation: "Higher Ground" by Stevie Wonder
9. 1 gift can be exchanged now (or wait until Jan 1st)

30TH
CROWN ROYAL

Crown Royal - To make our collective vocation the building and developing of our community in order to restore our people to their traditional greatness. Pursuit of a common **purpose**.

(light a red or green candle)

1. Host a get together or celebrate solo.
2. Choose someone to be the MC. (If possible, choose the oldest person)
3. The MC prays for everyone.
4. Huddle up and say "Crown Me!"
5. The MC pours out a little liquor (or water)
6. The MC directs the youngest person to use the black candle to light the next candle.
7. Discuss the proof of black excellence, in all forms, from past until present, choose a goal for the year, tell a story, read an excerpt from a book or publication, sing or listen to a song.
8. 1 gift can be exchanged now (or wait until Jan 1st)

31ST

KUUMBA

Kuumba - To always do as much as we can, in the way we can, in order to leave our community more beautiful and beneficial than we inherited it. Use our **Creativity.** (light a red or green candle)

1. Gather everyone together.
2. Eldest person (or leader): "Habari gani?" (what's happening?)
3. Everyone: "Kuumba!"
4. Pray
5. Everyone: "Harambe!" (let's pull together!)
6. Pour out libations
7. The youngest uses the black candle to light the next candle on the Kinara.
8. Discuss Kuumba, tell a story, read an excerpt from a book or publication, sing or listen to a song.
   Song Recommendation: "Nan Sira Madi" by Ballake Sissoko
9. 1 gift can be exchanged now (or wait until Jan 1st)
10. This is the day The Great Feast can occur.

31ST

HELLA SMART

Hella Smart - To always do as much as we can, in the way we can, in order to leave our community more beautiful and beneficial than we inherited it. Use our **Creativity.**

(light a red or green candle)

1. Host a get together or celebrate solo.
2. Choose someone to be the MC. (If possible, choose the oldest person)
3. The MC prays for everyone.
4. Huddle up and say "You know how we do!"
5. The MC pours out a little liquor (or water)
6. The MC directs the youngest person to use the black candle to light the next candle.
7. Discuss the things we want to do in-house or in-community, planning possibilities, choose a goal for the year, tell a story, read an excerpt from a book or publication, sing or listen to a song.
8. 1 gift can be exchanged now (or wait until Jan 1st)

1ST

IMANI

Imani - To believe with all our heart in ourselves, our people, our parents, our teachers, our leaders, and the righteousness and victory of our struggle. Become established and rooted in **Faith.** (light remaining candle)

1. Gather everyone together.
2. Eldest person (or leader): "Habari gani?" (what's happening?)
3. Everyone: "Imani!"
4. Pray
5. Everyone: "Harambe!" (let's pull together!)
6. Pour out libations
7. The youngest uses the black candle to light the next candle on the Kinara.
8. Discuss Imani, tell a story, read an excerpt from a book or publication, sing or listen to a song.
   Song Recommendation: "Don't Lose Your Steam" by Gregory Porter
9. Exchange gifts (preferably made by hand)

1ST
COME HELL OR HIGH WATER

Come hell or high water- To believe with all our heart in ourselves, our people, our parents, our teachers, our leaders, and the righteousness and victory of our struggle. Become established and rooted in **Faith.**

(light remaining candle)

1. Host a get together or celebrate solo.
2. Choose someone to be the MC. (If possible, choose the oldest person)
3. The MC prays for everyone.
4. Huddle up and say "Never back down!"
5. The MC pours out a little liquor (or water)
6. The MC directs the youngest person to use the black candle to light the last candle.
7. Use this time to talk about the victories so far, celebrate the wins, share the names of the grassroots movements, uplift each other and community leaders, tell a story, read an excerpt from a book, social media or publication, sing or listen to a song.
8. Gift exchange day. (preferably homemade)
10. Eat together.

RECIPES

Hot Water Cornbread with Aubergine épicée (spicy eggplant)

Hot Water Cornbread

Ingredients
- 2 cups self-rising cornmeal
- 1 1/2 to 2 cups boiling water
- pinch of salt (optional)
- avocado oil for frying

Instructions
- Pour about 1/2 inch of oil into a heavy-bottomed skillet. Heat the oil to about 350° or until glistening but not smoking. In a large glass or metal bowl combine the self-rising corn meal with about 1 cup of boiling water. Carefully stir to combine. The batter should be a thick consistency. A bit wetter than bread dough. Add additional water or cornmeal until you reach the consistency of thick batter that doesn't lose shape when you remove the spoon. Different corn meals will require different amounts of water. Start with less and add more if you need it.
- Once the oil is hot, scoop about 1/4 cup of the batter into palm of your hand (careful, hot!). Shape into rounded patties. Place carefully into the oil using a spatula. Cook 3 to 5 minutes or until brown around the edges then carefully flip over and cook an additional 3 to 4 minutes. Work in batches, adding additional oil if necessary. Drain the cornbread on a plate lined with paper towels. Serve warm.

Aubergine épicée

Ingredients
- 1 medium aubergine (eggplant)
- 1 small onion
- 1 tomato
- garlic cloves
- 1 bay leaf
- 1/2 bunch parsley
- 2 tbs avocado oil
- red pepper flakes, black pepper, sea salt
- 1 habanero
- avocado oil for frying
- 1/2 cup vegetable stock (or chicken stock or seafood stock)

Instructions
Dice and chop all of the vegetables, except for the habanero, and cook in a heavy-bottomed skillet or saucepan. Heat the oil to about 350° or until glistening but not smoking. After 5 minutes, drop the whole habanero into the pan along with the spices and seasonings and bay leaf. Pour in the stock. If you like a looser sauce, add more stock. If you like a thicker sauce allow it to simmer on low until desired consistency. Cook for about 35 minutes, stirring occasionally to prevent the bottom from sticking. Discard the habanero and bay leaf before serving.

RECIPES

Aloco (ripened & fried plantain)

Ingredients:
4 ripened plantain
1/2 cup avocado oil

Directions:
Peel the ripe plantain. Cut lengthwise in half. Cut the two halves again lengthwise. Cut the four slices into bite size pieces about the width of a thumb. Heat oil to 400 degrees and fry the plantain until they caramelize and darken. Place on a cooling rack and let rest for 5 minutes.

Spicy Pickled Purple Cabbage and Beets

Ingredients:
1 purple cabbage
3 small beets
1 tsp himalayan salt
3 dehydrated red chili peppers
2 minced garlic cloves
1/2 cup apple cider vinegar
1/2 cup water
canning jar or glass container with a lid

Directions:
Wash and slice the cabbage and beets and place in the jar with the garlic and chopped up red chili peppers. Pour in the water and vinegar. This is not for fermenting. Allow to marinate in the refrigerator for at least a day. Open and enjoy as a condiment to greens, fish, chicken and more.

RECIPES

Black Eyed Peas and Collard Greens with Okra

Ingredients:
1/2 lb fresh frozen black eyed peas
1 lb collard greens
10 oz fresh okra
3 cloves garlic
1 tomato
1 shallot
1 small yellow onion
1 green pepper
1 anaheim pepper
2 tsp himalayan salt, black pepper, red pepper, tumeric
olive oil
4 cups chicken stock (or water if you want it to be vegan)

Directions:
Warm some olive oil on low heat. Do not allow to become smoky. Dice the tomato, shallot, yellow onion, green pepper, anaheim pepper and garlic. Put all of the diced vegetables in the olive oil for 8 minutes to soften. Wash and trim the collards and okra. Toss into a big pot along with the defrosted black eyed peas. Add the cooked diced vegetables and pour in 4 cups of chicken stock and stir in your spices. Cook for 2 hours on low heat.

Oxtails and lima beans

Ingredients:
1 pkg oxtails (appx 6-8 pieces)
1 onion & garlic
salt & black pepper & garlic powder
2 tsp all spice, 2 bay leaves
1 tomato
lima beans
water

Directions:
Place the whole peeled onion and garlic, the halved tomato, spices, bay leaf and beans in a pot with 6 cups of water. Season the oxtails with salt and pepper and brown on all sides in a cast iron skillet before adding to the pot with the beans. Cover and cook on low for 4 hours. Be sure to check water level. Season to taste.

RECIPES

Sweet Potato Pie

Ingredients:
2 cups cooked, mashed sweet potatoes
1 ¼ cup turbinado sugar
½ tsp nutmeg
1 ¼ tsp ground cinnamon
11 tbs room temperature butter diced or sliced
2 large eggs
2 tsp Maya's vanilla extract
1 unbaked pie crust
¼ tsp salt plus a pinch

Directions:
Be sure to remove any stringiness from the mashed sweet potatoes. Mix all of the ingredients together and pour into the pie crust. Bake on 350 degrees for 45-55 minutes. Allow to cool for an hour, then refrigerate until ready to eat.

GIFTS TO MAKE AND EAT

For Adults

Maya's Vanilla Extract

Materials:

5	4oz canning jars with lids
10	vanilla beans
20oz	Black Momma Unflavored Vodka (or an 80 proof brand of your choice)

Instructions:

1. Place two vanilla beans per jar
2. Fill each jar with vodka
3. Place the lids on and store out of the sunlight
4. Wait at least 8 weeks (best in 6-12 months)
5. You can continue to refill with vodka over time adding more vanilla beans if you like or pouring into a larger canning jar for larger quantities. (appx. 5 vanilla beans per 8oz vodka.

GIFTS THAT KEEP GIVING

A Coat of Arms

Materials:
Canva or another digital platform
Family Crest Template

Instructions:
1. pull up the template
2. choose the colors
3. choose the symbols
4. write the manifesto
5. save it and post it to social media
6. everyone sign/comment underneath or print and mount to hang.

REFLECTIONS

Holidays of varying kinds may very well have originated centuries or decades ago, but, none of it becomes important to us unless we feel connected to it. Take a moment and reflect back through your years. Through remembering your own experiences, you may recognize that your choice to continue (or not) with a given tradition was based on your emotional memories. Consider that, once you were grown, you had the freedom to choose how you wanted to spend time off. Any vacation, time of rest and recovery, rejuvenation and reflection were precious. It is my sincerest hope that, by now, you have elected to only participate in the things that are meaningful to you.

Secondly, the very nature of any observance, celebration or remembrance rooted in the days of old had been to amplify the culture, or country, the environment and timeframe. Those celebrations were to help ground a people and make room to allow for an overflow of gratitude, grief, hope and so much more. To embrace the traditions of old, we only need to look at the seasons and cycles of humanity and life, climate and the heavens. It is in this space we will find what we now call...

Holiday

As I reflected on my knowledge of partying and joyful celebrations and how they were in my family, I quickly threw aside my desire to scream and rant about how much the typical December holidays needed to change. Instead, I found myself shedding tears of joy as my heart was filled with hope. After 12 years of trial and error with my own household and children, I began to recognize a trend within our expressions after holiday times came to a close:

We all enjoyed being together and longed for more, sometimes it felt boring, sometimes there were disagreements and pettiness.

My children disliked shopping, and they often found it difficult to find the right thing to buy because they didn't have the money to do so. I, admittedly, found the season to be my most melancholy as I longed to see relatives who had crossed over out of this human experience. On top of that, I also remembered my childhood days of receiving a brown box ceremoniously brought from the church by the Pastor, Deacon or Youth Minister with toys because my family was on "the list". With time, I became ashamed because they never visited us any other time of the year. During our holiday dinners there were often conversations at the table that sparked controversy. Naturally, we also had conversations that brought healing and laughter.

The most surprising and fulfilling times were those that allowed us to tap into the stories of lives well lived (or tragically so) by grandparents, grand-aunts and grand-uncles, the neighborhood, life and how we were of service and a reflection of our community. Time together stopped for a few hours and we all connected. The typical holidays were only inadequate when I desired to celebrate like I saw in the commercials or in the movies and books I'd consumed over time. However, when I focused on our personal intentions and our mindfulness in preparation of the holiday season, my joy was limitless.

Over the course of 2020 and 2021, it had become very obvious to me that we would all eventually get back to real life and lose the forced "slow-down and stay home" situations the global pandemic imparted. Although I have new introvert tendencies, my desire to create a more meaningful way of enjoying holiday time rages on at a level significantly higher than it has in prior years. I want to spend time rejoicing in a way that is meaningful and allows space for me to no longer take for granted the experiences, the people, the family, the opportunities, and the community surrounding me. I decidedly thought:

I want to establish traditions of the heart that will be little seeds planted in the souls of my children and with watering and nurturing, become giant trees that bear fruit and shade for their life's journey.

With this in mind, I cycled through a few holidays and their practices in an attempt to expose my children to something more meaningful. Eventually, I arrived to a Kwanzaa despite my previous attitude where I had proclaimed that it was a "dumb, made-up" holiday.

Honestly, since 2019, I have celebrated National Hot Dog Day, Coffee Day, Best Friend Day and National Hang Outside and Meet a Neighbor Day. I participated in Donut Day, Yoga Day, Flashback Friday and Hug a Cat day.

Any reason to celebrate, right?

While it is true that Kwanzaa has its origins in the United States in the 1960s by a man whose personal life was called into question years after his release of the holiday tenets. The daily principles are not to be overshadowed by intentional social pressure to trivialize African American (black chattel slave) history, culture and experience.

Over the years, I had heard of Kwanzaa and had even celebrated one day in the household of a friend who lived in Southfield, Michigan. Growing up in Detroit where the African Diaspora had major roots and foundations well established, I was surprised to think back to my adolescent years and recall feeling like only "bourgeoisie (a..k.a boujee) black people" celebrated Kwanzaa. After all, we had family who ascribed to Black Nationalist thought, were part of the Black Hebrew Israelite belief, had connections to Black Moors, Black Panthers and more. My knowledge of Kwanzaa was lacking in a tremendous way. As I sought to pull together my first Kwanzaa celebration for my household, I felt a huge sense of inadequacy.

I felt the despondency in my heart that resulted from my years of pursuing inclusion and assimilation into the white American culture. I had trained myself to learn how to fit in socially, deny my hearts' calling and desires in an effort to temper my blackness. As a light skinned black woman, I also dared not veer too far off course and risk losing my black card all together at the hands of my cousins. As I think back, the very act of gathering the symbolic materials for the celebration tempted me to feel self conscious. I could not find a place to learn what to do on each of the 7 days of the celebration, candles in the colors I needed were hard to find, and where or where would I find an appropriate candelabra?

As a result, I created a book with a modified compilation of the information I found scattered around on the internet, my family recipes, gift ideas to make by hand and plenty of workspace and guidance to help design and keep record of an African American made tradition that could be adopted and individualized as our own. Again, I decidedly thought:

A holiday more suited for my true soulfulness.

My family and I agree that we find the daily s more in line with how we choose to live our lives these days.

Although I am American, living as Black in America has allowed me to filter life through a different lens. We practice mindfulness and intention setting in addition to our faith-based beliefs and, therefore, find Kwanzaa's Principles of Unity, Self-Determination, Collective Work and Responsibility, Cooperative Economics, Purpose, Creativity and Faith have room to become grand anchors for our hearts. Consequently, it presents as a perfect way to lasso the crap storm that has been occurring inside or outside of our household and communities. We refuse to submit to the trend of chaotic culture and divided living.

Kwanzaa is a way forward to our future for post-pandemic recovery.

Unity and a codex

Now more than ever, across the past several months, divisive language, fighting, contention, clamoring to gain a better financial foothold and polarizing beliefs have taken precedence. Flat out lies and denial that systemic racism existed and currently exists is debated among us in the 6th Region of Africa here in the Americas.

Colorism, interpersonal violence and scarcity of resources wreak havoc on us and is a threat to our foundation as a collective. Conversely, there has been a collective rise in self awareness, desire for healing, clamoring for knowledge and support for transforming trauma, hurt and health, while sharing ideas for uplifting and increasing love. We are unequivocally pronouncing and announcing the dignified and majestic fundamental differences Black People posses in their being.

We are in transformative times!

The wave of change that is occurring is ripe opportunity for a loud voice to cry out for unity. I see no better way to support this effort than by implementing a celebration that reflects culture, timeframe, history and ancestral remembrance, spirituality, stewardship of resources, value for every human life and hope.

I no longer ascribe to a belief that Kwanzaa is somehow inferior to celebrating any other tradition. So, go ahead and enjoy Christmas, celebrate Hanukkah or New Year's Day if that is your preference. They are not mutually exclusive of Kwanzaa.

WE are ready to party.

Yet, more than that, we are ready to reimagine our collective joy and purpose. We are ready to listen and to laugh, to pour out libations in honor of our ancestors, to debate and pray over our connections and responsibility to one another, economics and our individual greatness as we share a meal. We plan to document our gatherings in a family codex, to revisit it and pass it down with honor.

This is now our annual tradition.

PERSONAL REFLECTIONS

PERSONAL REFLECTIONS

PERSONAL
REFLECTIONS

PERSONAL REFLECTIONS

PERSONAL REFLECTIONS

PERSONAL REFLECTIONS

PERSONAL REFLECTIONS

CHEERS TO AN ANNUAL TRADITION!

MOJA!   KUJICHAGULIA!   UJIMA!   UJAMAA!   NIA!   KUUMBA!   IMANI!

Coat of Arms

Design a Coat of Arms that represents your heritage, interests and hobbies.

NAME OURSELVES

NAME INDEX

Name:
meaning:
reason chosen:
history of the name:
nickname:

Name:
meaning:
reason chosen:
history of the name:
nickname:

Name:
meaning:
reason chosen:
history of the name:
nickname:

Name:
meaning:
reason chosen:
history of the name:
nickname:

GOVERNMENT HACKS

FAMILY TREE

TKE

photo here

UNC'S RECOMMENDATIONS

1.learning

2.travel/transportation

3.eating

4.relationships

5.celebrating

TKE

photo here

AIN'TIE'S RECOMMENDATIONS

1.learning

2.travel/transportation

3.eating

4.relationships

5.celebrating

RESOURCES

Amsterdam News, Dec 26, 2017, *Kwanzaa: An African- American Cultural Celebration*, Retrieved from: http://amsterdamnews.com/news/2017/dec/26/kwanzaa-an-african-american-cultural-celebration/

Bechi, Maya. (Oct 22. 2021). *Kwanzaa: A Holiday for Mindfulness?,* Retrieved from: mayabechi.medium.com

Bechi, Maya. 2021. All Recipes belong to the author.

Canva, 2022, Stock photos

National Museum of African American History and Culture, *The Seven Principles of Kwanzaa*, Retrieved from: https://nmaahc.si.edu/blog-post/seven-principles-kwanzaa

www.ingramcontent.com/pod-product-compliance
Lightning Source LLC
Chambersburg PA
CBHW052118020426
42335CB00021B/2812